Laughing Stock

Laughing Stock

A Cow's Guide To Life

Texas Bix Bender

GIBBS·SMITH
PUBLISHER
Salt Lake City

99 98 97   15 14 13 12 11 10 9 8 7 6

This is a Peregrine Smith Book, published by
Gibbs Smith, Publisher
P.O. Box 667
Layton, Utah 84041

Design by Mary Ellen Thompson
Illustrations by Bonnie Cazier: pages 14, 18, 20, 22, 34, 48,
62, 72, 82, 94, 112, 118, 134, 136, 100, 140
Illustrations by Calvin Grondahl: pages 8, 12, 16, 28, 30, 36,
38, 42, 44, 54, 58, 60, 66, 70, 74, 76, 78, 80, 88, 90, 92, 96,
98, 108, 110, 116, 120, 122, 124, 128, 130, 132, 138
Illustrations by Steve Egan: pages 6, 10, 24, 26, 32, 40, 46,
50, 52, 56, 64, 68, 84, 86, 102, 106, 114, 126, 142
Corner animation: Dave Holl

Cover background courtesy Tandy Leather Company,
Roy, Ut.

Printed and bound in the United States of America

Library of Congress Cataloging-in-Publication Data
Bender, Texas Bix, 1949-
Laughing stock : a cow's guide to life / Texas Bix Bender.
    p.   cm.
  ISBN 0-87905-630-4 (pbk.)
  1. Cows—Humor. 2. Conduct of life—Humor. I. Title.
  PN6231.C24B46   1994
818'5402–dc20   93-48165
                                    CIP

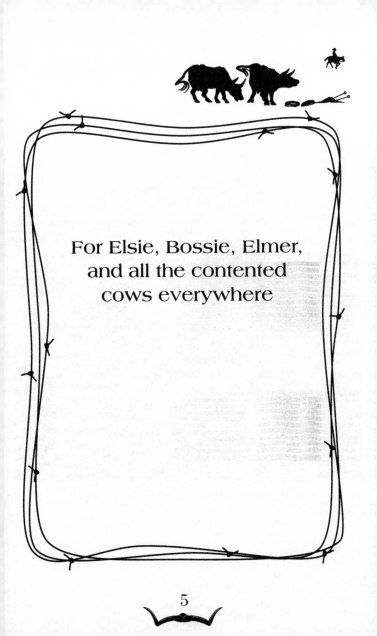

For Elsie, Bossie, Elmer,
and all the contented
cows everywhere

5

They made
tomorrow
so you wouldn't
have to eat
everything today.

Worrying is like standing in a mud hole; it gives you something to do, but it doesn't get you anywhere.

Sometimes
the only way
to grab a bull
by the horns
is to slap on
the hobbles.

9

If you wait
by the gate,
it will open.

Good grazing
makes those who
are there happy,
and attracts those
who are far off.

11

There are more
horses' patoots
than horses.

The sun does not rise
to hear the
rooster crow.

Moo low,
moo slow,
and don't
moo too much.

— Duke Longhorn

"Weighs a ton,
eyes of dun,
Could she, could she,
could she moo,
Has anybody seen
my cow?"

Let us honor
if we can
the vertical cow,
Though we
value none
but the
slaughtered one.

— W. H. Aberdeen

No flies
can enter a
closed mouth.

Some shoo flies;
others let them
go barefoot.

19

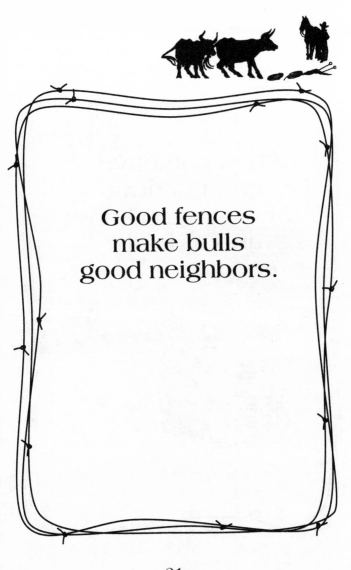

Good fences
make bulls
good neighbors.

21

When you have a
cud to chew,
how can you know
about death?

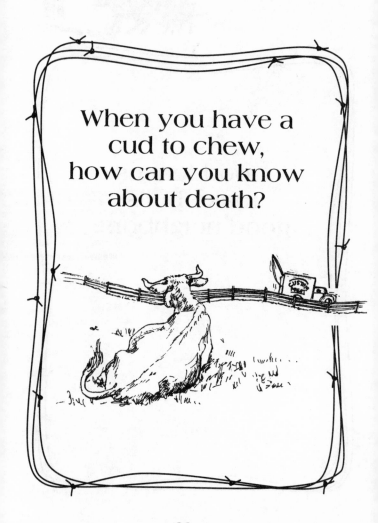

Don't have a cow
unless you
are a cow.

Even the poorest
cow has a
leather coat.

The easiest
relationship is to be
a part of the herd.
The hardest is to be
apart from it.

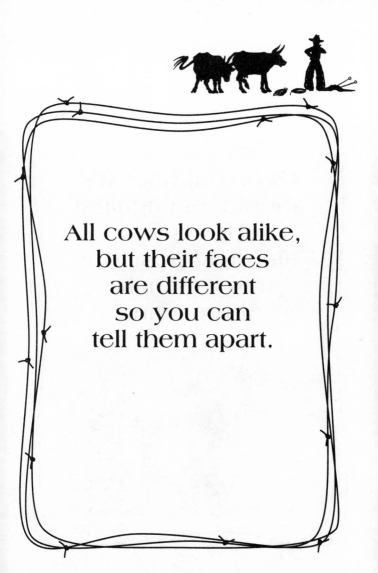

All cows look alike,
but their faces
are different
so you can
tell them apart.

27

Overweight cows
should rest against
objects in a
standing position;
this will make
them lean.

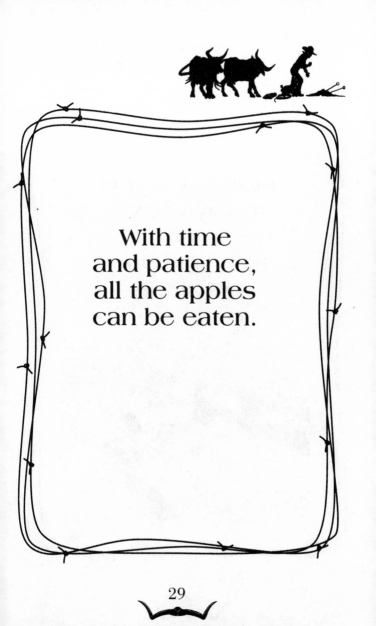

With time
and patience,
all the apples
can be eaten.

Feast and you
always have
company.
Fast and you
fast alone.

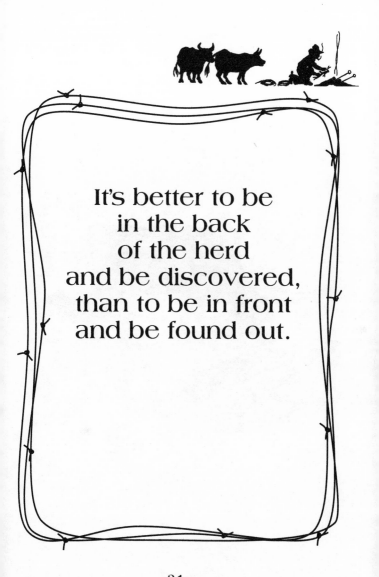

It's better to be
in the back
of the herd
and be discovered,
than to be in front
and be found out.

31

A river
can't be measured
with a taste.

Keep your face
to the sun
and the shadows
will fall
behind you.

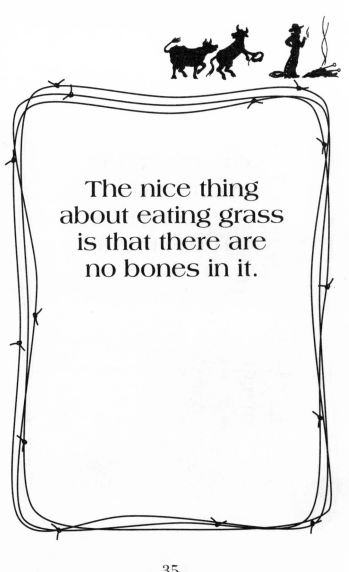

The nice thing
about eating grass
is that there are
no bones in it.

When you find
yourself in
over your head,
don't open your
mouth.
Swim!

Let the cow
into paradise
and leave the
bull behind.

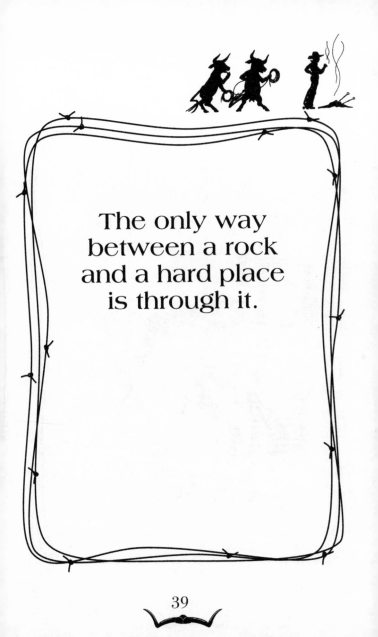

The only way
between a rock
and a hard place
is through it.

To a cow,
every day is just
an udder day.

If you're approaching
Land's End,
you need a
cattle-log.

A little music
in the barn
puts a cow
in the mooood.

It's easy
to be content
with your lot
if it's a feed lot.

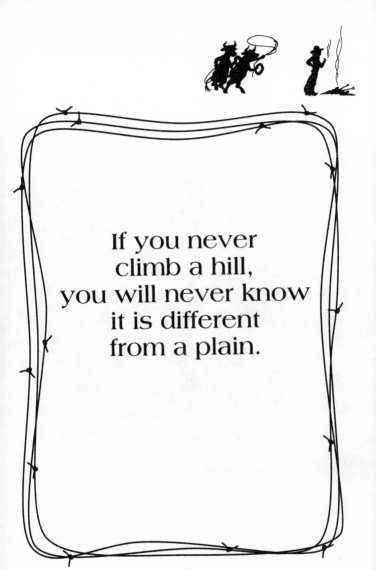

If you never
climb a hill,
you will never know
it is different
from a plain.

46

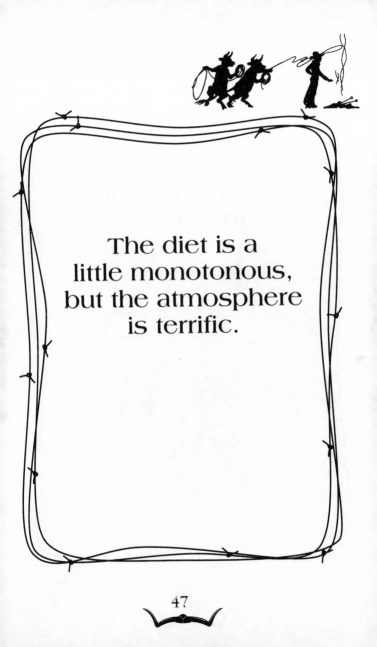

The diet is a
little monotonous,
but the atmosphere
is terrific.

To err is human;
therefore,
cows can do
no wrong.

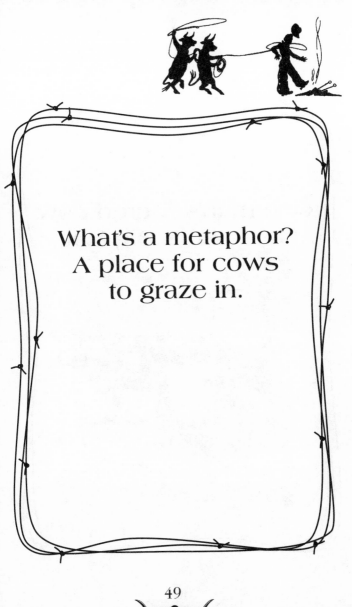

What's a metaphor?
A place for cows
to graze in.

One man's sacred cow is another's Big Mac.

Cows have their faults,
but eating meat
isn't one of them.

Even an old cow
deserves a
new cowbell.

Never play
leapfrog
with a bull.

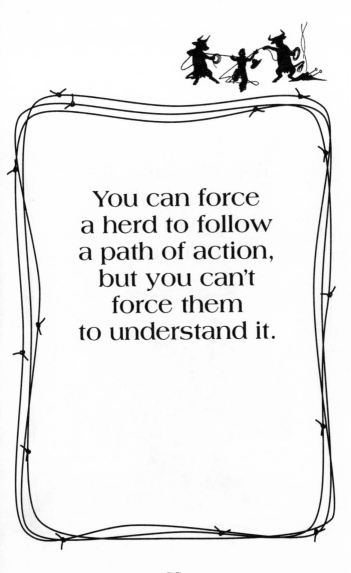

You can force
a herd to follow
a path of action,
but you can't
force them
to understand it.

You can always
tell a bull,
but you can't
tell him much.

Change the
environment;
don't try to
change the cow.

— Buckminster Bull

There is nothing
like lying
on your belly
in soft,
cool mud.

"Laughing Stock."

There are hundreds
of uses
for cowhide,
but the most
important
is to hold
the cow together.

You can lead
a cow to fodder,
but you can't
make her think.

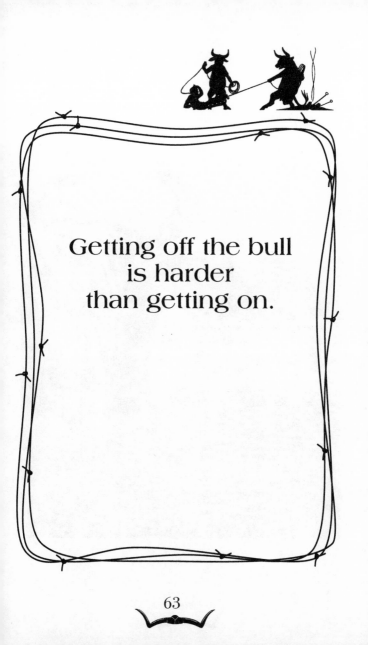

Getting off the bull
is harder
than getting on.

It's better to cross
the muddy ground
to the hay,
than to stand
and long
to be there.

If faced with a
choice between
an open gate
and a bale of hay,
take the hay.

A herd is
the result
of love in bloom.

I once went all day
without food and
all night without
sleep to enable me
to think. It was a
waste of time.
Cows can't think.
— Tao of Moo

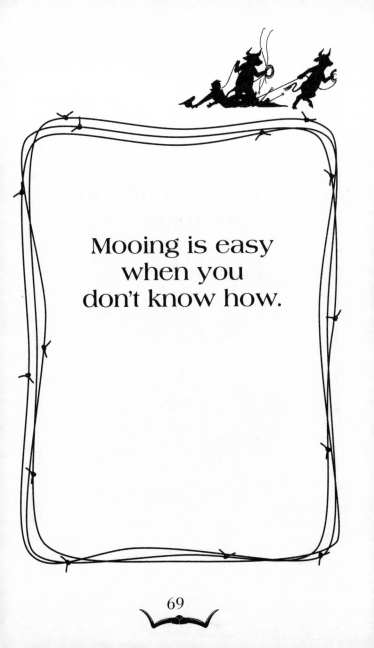

Mooing is easy
when you
don't know how.

Two heads are not
better than one,
but two
stomachs are.

GIHO —
Grass in,
hamburger out.

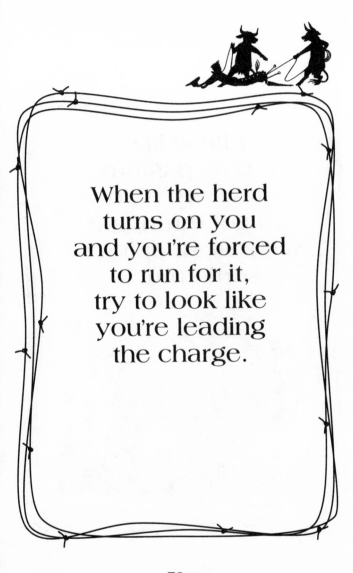

When the herd
turns on you
and you're forced
to run for it,
try to look like
you're leading
the charge.

Life is like
a cow pasture.
It's very hard
to get through it
without stepping in
some muck.

If you can
keep your head
while all about you
are losing theirs,
you obviously
don't understand
the situation.

It's not true
that life is just
one darn thing
after another.
It's the same
darn thing
over and over.

The bridges you cross
before you come
to them
are usually
over rivers
that aren't there.

Weight
and brands
are hard to hide.

When you have to
hobble a cow,
a little grain
softens the misery.

On a clear day
you can
moo forever.

There's nothing like
a stable environment
to make a
cow contented.

Being stubborn
is the only way
to stand out
in a herd.

A change of pasture
can lead to
a fatter calf.

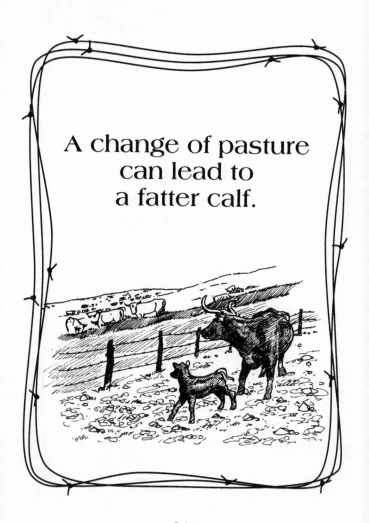

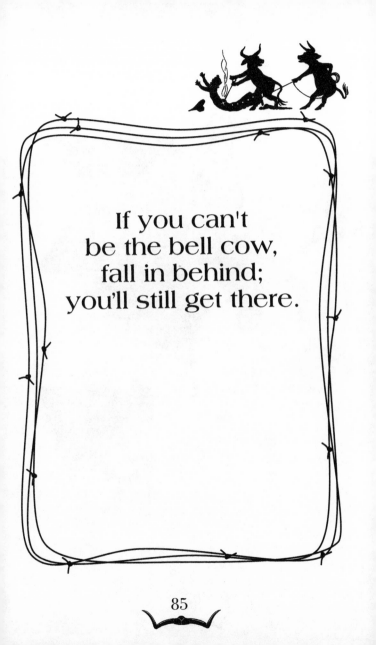

If you can't
be the bell cow,
fall in behind;
you'll still get there.

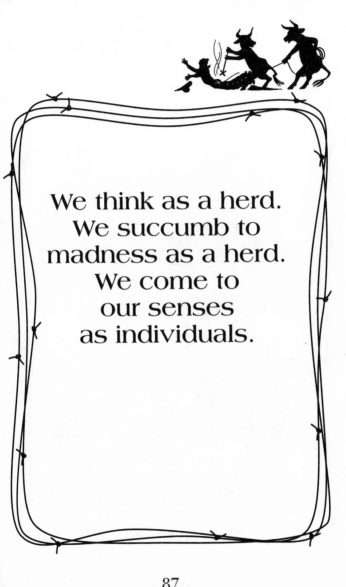

We think as a herd.
We succumb to
madness as a herd.
We come to
our senses
as individuals.

When you get up to look, you lose your place.

The world
doesn't mind
a clever cow,
as long as
the cow
is the only one
who knows.

89

Bulls seldom
make passes
at heifers
with gases.

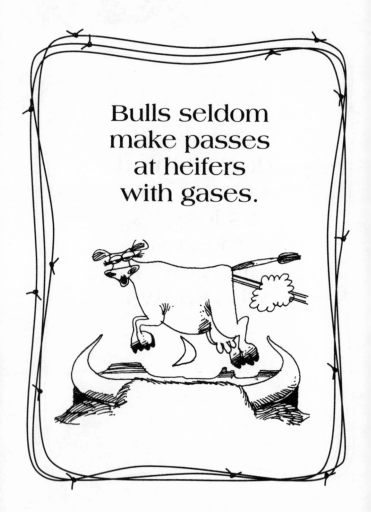

There are many
contented cows,
but who has heard
of a contented
rancher?

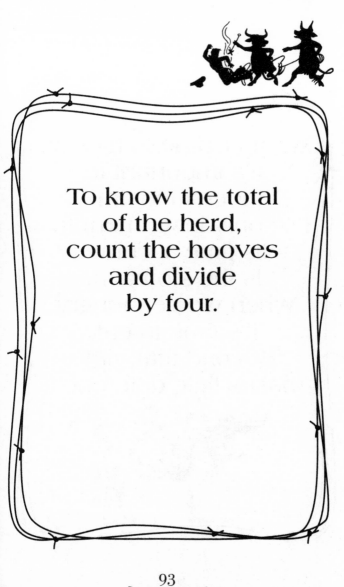

To know the total
of the herd,
count the hooves
and divide
by four.

What is Time to a Cow?
It's important to
understand time.
The only instrument that
tells time accurately
is the stomach.
When we get hungry,
it's time to eat.
Beyond that, time
makes little difference.

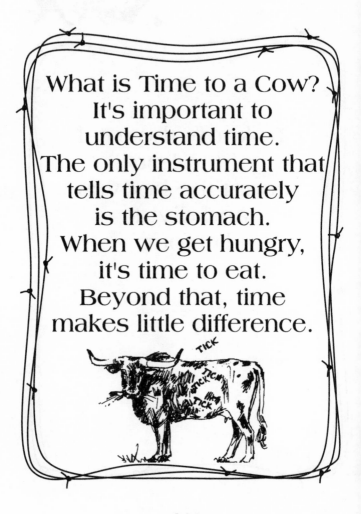

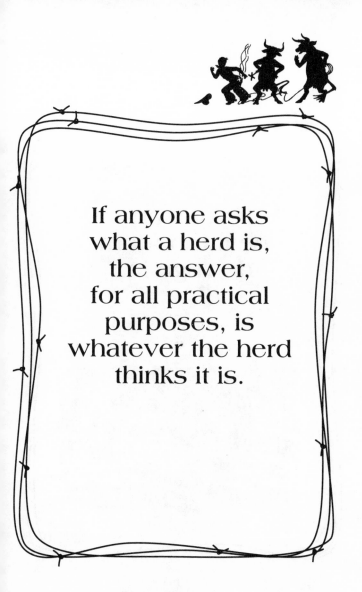

If anyone asks
what a herd is,
the answer,
for all practical
purposes, is
whatever the herd
thinks it is.

If you can't
see the bottom,
don't go in.

Not even a cow
wants to stay
barefoot
and pregnant.

A good bowel
is worth more
than any amount
of brains.

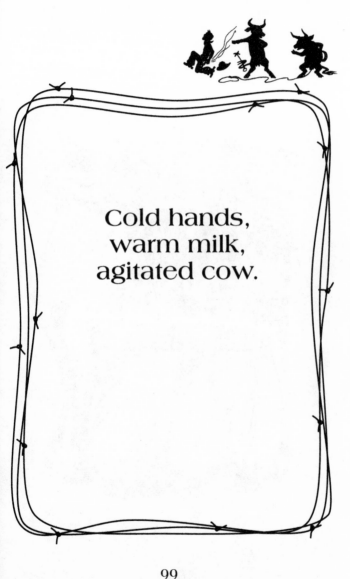

Cold hands,
warm milk,
agitated cow.

Before the flowers
of friendship fade,
eat them.

— Gertrude Holstein

Waiting for Godot.

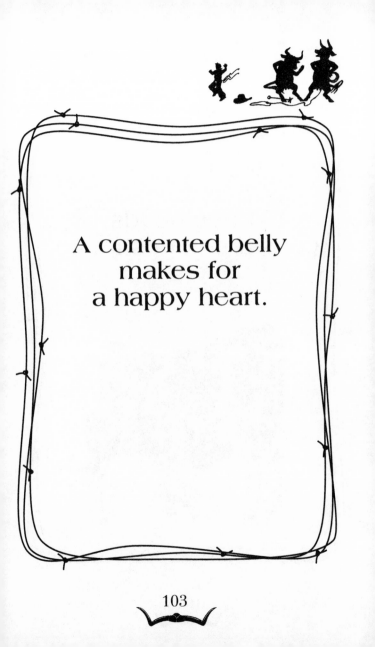

A contented belly
makes for
a happy heart.

Love needs
constant nourishment.

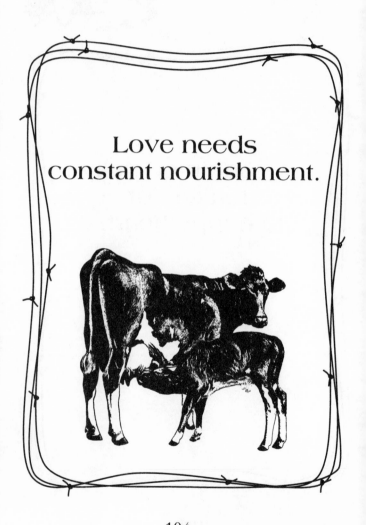

Get all the fools
on your side
and you can
lead the herd.

When shade
is sparse,
it must be shared.

Where have all the
flowers gone?
Cows ate them
every one.
When will they
ever learn?
When will they
ever learn?

The thousand-mile
trail drive
ends with
the last step.

Don't eat anything
that has a
face on it.

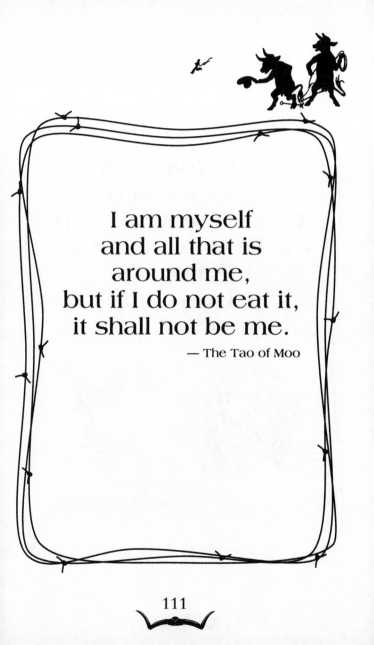

I am myself
and all that is
around me,
but if I do not eat it,
it shall not be me.

— The Tao of Moo

111

There may come
a day when
the cow and the lion
will lie down together,
but the cow
won't get
much sleep.

If you're being
chased by a bull
while you're
milking the cow,
go ahead and
milk the cow;
you can always
shoot the bull.

Every tail
has an end.

Two's company, three's a herd.

Know your limits
or you'll find
yourself
all hobbled up
with everywhere
to go.

If you have to
run for it,
do so
before you have to.

It's better to remove
a bull's horns
all at once,
rather than
an inch at a time.

If you're
following a cow,
you should know
that in all likelihood,
it too
is following a cow.

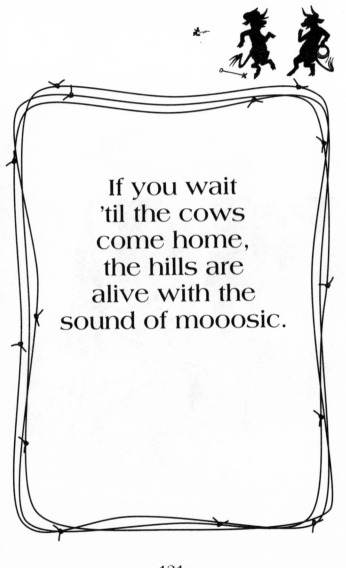

If you wait
'til the cows
come home,
the hills are
alive with the
sound of mooosic.

A cow chip
is a picnic
to a fly.

123

A herd of a thousand cows begins with a single bull.

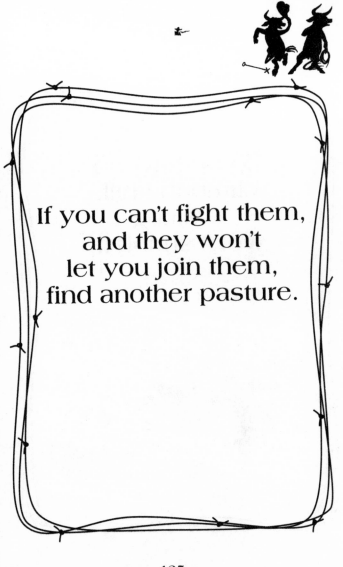

If you can't fight them,
and they won't
let you join them,
find another pasture.

If you have to
climb the hill,
waiting
won't shrink it.

Those who know
don't talk.
Those who talk
don't know.
Those who moo, do.

Swatting flies is a
thankless job,
but nonetheless
important.

When the soul
lies down
in fresh,
sweet grass,
the world is
too full
to talk about.

Never do anything
you can't moo about
after dinner.

Oom
is moo
backwards.

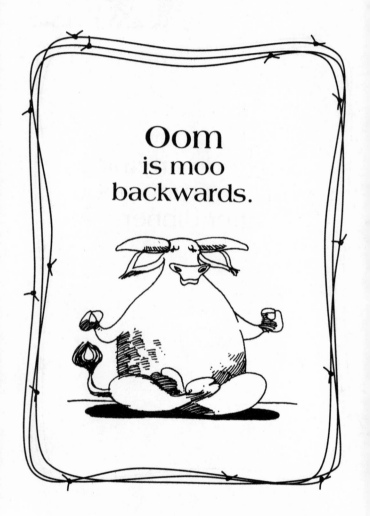

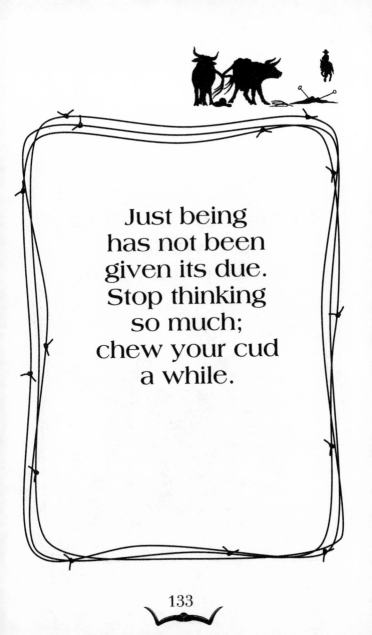

Just being
has not been
given its due.
Stop thinking
so much;
chew your cud
a while.

Nothing is so ordinary as wanting to be remarkable.

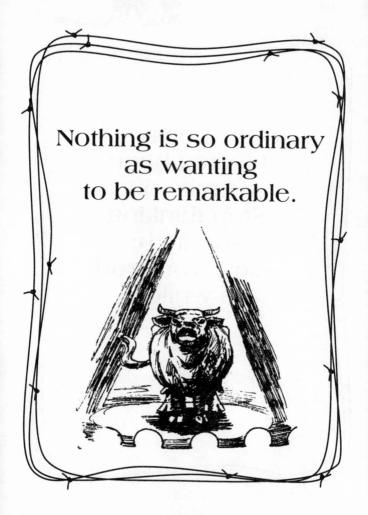

You can cover it
with sugar
and bake
it in the oven,
but a cowpie
is still manure.

Anyone
concerned about
their dignity
should make
a point
never to ride a bull.

If you straddle
the fence,
you'll never have your
feet on the ground.

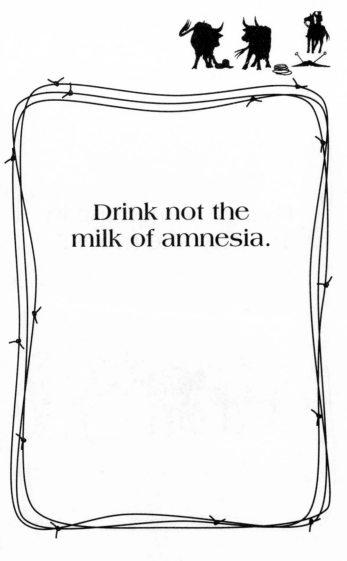

Drink not the
milk of amnesia.

"There's something in the way she moos."

The path
continuously followed
becomes a habit.

It ain't over
till the
fat cow sings!